T0365330

CAT TALES

KITTY CAPERS AND MORE

Written and illustrated by
LaVera Edick

Order this book online at www.trafford.com
or email orders@trafford.com

Most Trafford titles are also available at major online book retailers.

Print information available on the last page.

ISBN: 978-1-4907-6651-5 (softcover)
        978-1-4907-6652-2 (ebook)
        978-1-4907-6791-8 (audio)

Library of Congress Control Number: 2015917770

Our mission is to efficiently provide the world's finest, most comprehensive book publishing service, enabling every author to experience
success. To find out how to publish your book, your way, and have it available worldwide, visit us online at www.trafford.com

Trafford rev. 02/12/2016

www.trafford.com

North America & international
toll-free: 1 888 232 4444 (USA & Canada)
fax: 812 355 4082

DEDICATION

CAT TALES KITTY CAPERS AND MORE is dedicated to the memory of my "other mother" Ruth, who shared her home and love with an adopted feline family; also to my parents, Ray and Minnie Woodring, who allowed me to have pet dogs and cats, teaching me responsibility and love. My mother captured special moments of her children with their pets by taking pictures with her Brownie Kodak camera.

Thanks to Jackie Glenn for painstakingly editing my book. She was a great help.

Thanks to Vern Skaug, a long-time friend and teacher, for all of his help.

FOREWORD

In the winter years of my life, and at 90 years of age, I am writing and illustrating my second book- CAT TALES KITTY CAPERS AND MORE. Part One of the book is a story of Ruth and the feline family of four that she adopted, or did they adopt her? The story evolved from her weekly letters to me and her daily journals. Her feline family filled the senior years of her life with adventure and love. It began when a half-starved stray cat came to her door. Against her better judgment she fed "him" and fell in love with not "him" but a very pregnant "her". Ruth named her Lady and was very disappointed when she disappeared. However, she was only gone for a few days when she returned bringing a gift, a tiny blue-grey kitten that she dropped at Ruth's feet. She would leave, but come back every day to feed her baby. It was a week later before she brought the second baby, then the third and the fourth. In Ruth's words "She must have been testing me to see if I would take good care of her first baby before she trusted me with the rest of her family."

The unconditional love of animals for their humans makes life more meaningful and less lonely in the winter years of our lives through companionship, love, a feeling of being needed and a sense of security and protection. Statistics tell us that the elderly live longer, happier lives when they have a pet. Love is the most important health attribute we have and pets are one of nature's best sources of love. Pets help us unwind and they can make us laugh and divert our minds away from troubles. Several recent studies have shown that having a pet to love can aid in relaxation and promote good health by reducing stress and reducing cholesterol and blood pressure levels. "Pets help reduce cortisol, a stress hormone, while boosting the same pain-easing, mood-lifting chemical you experience when you are in love." explains a well-known psychologist; and that happy feeling delivers another benefit- your resistance to germs.

Part two, AND MORE, is about pets in my family and paintings I have done of them over the years. My parents realized the importance of pets in their children's lives as a way of teaching them responsibility and an appreciation for the love shared between them and their pets. The photos my mother took of my brother, Harold (ca 1920) with his Collie, Carlos, and of me and my cat, Bluey (ca 1925), were the source of the paintings in my book. Photos of my paintings tell stories of pets in the lives of my children, grandchildren, great grandchildren and of my great, great grandchild.

Dogs and cats are the most popular pets; however there certainly are many others: Horses, pigs, rabbits, goats, birds and even snakes have been noted to be very devoted to their owners.

I have included photos and stories of working dogs in AND MORE: Champ, who works with autistic children and Mimi, who is a "Pet Therapy Pal" working dog. Mimi visits hospitals and nursing homes to brighten the day for patients and residents. Studies have shown that surgical patients who cuddle with a pet after surgery needed 50% less pain medication. When you interact with an animal you love, your body receives a rush of pain-relieving endorphin.

Just as Ruth's feline family contributed to her health and happiness in the later years of her life, so does my faithful canine companion, Tousie, add love, happiness and a sense of being needed to the winter years of my life.

ACKNOWLEDGEMENTS

To Mathew and Janice for the photo and story about their pet pig, Leadbelly.

To Anne Carlsen Center for the photo and story about their working dog, Champ.

To Arlene for the photo and story about Pearl.

To Rita and Dane for photos and stories about their "Pet Therapy Pal" named Mimi.

I acknowledge use of statements made from studies that have been done about pets and how they enrich our lives, including:

AARP Magazine

Cardiologist Stephen Senalia, M.D.

Hope Reins, Inc

Psychologist Denee Jordon, Psy.D.

State University of New York, at Buffalo

University of California at Berkeley

CONTENTS

ILLUSTRATIONS

Chapter 1
LONELY

The days are long and I am so lonely since I lost my only child, Annalee, and then Andy, my friend for more than thirty years. I've been reminiscing and remembering the years I taught at the Birt Johnson County School, located four and a half miles north of our farm home where I grew up, near Stockville, Nebraska. From the home of one of my students, where I paid board and room, it took nearly an hour for me to walk to school, through cow pastures, over dirt roads and cornfields, in all kinds of weather. It kept me slim and trim! When snow drifts got waist high one of my brothers, Clarence or Earl, gave me a ride on horseback. I started teaching when I was only fifteen years old, but now my teaching career is behind me after more than fifty years of calling all of my little elementary students "my kids". I loved them all, but now those days are gone forever.

My beautiful red Mustang sits in my garage, "rarin' to go", but I just don't trust myself to lead it out into traffic as I once did. Perhaps I am becoming a hermit, or would an old lady be called a " hermitess"? I need someone to love; I love my back yard with the rock garden, the cat house, and the many tall, majestic oak trees, but I am still lonely. It isn't words of endearment I hear from the trees, it's only the wind whispering through their leaves. My rock garden is faithful, it is always there with the many cacti scattered among the volcanic rocks, warning me, "Don't get too close".

When Annalee died, I inherited her Toby and built the "cat house" for him here in the back yard of my Walnut Creek home. It is fancy, to say the least, complete with pet door, carpeting, cushioned beds and even a heating system.

Annalee loved her Toby so much. When I was living in Richmond and teaching school there, she rented an apartment on Knob Hill in San Francisco. Housing restrictions created a problem-- she couldn't keep her baby kitten, Toby, in the apartment. I had been keeping and caring for Toby for only a week when she somehow managed to get permission to keep her kitty—so—one Saturday morning I started out with Toby covered with a baby blanket. I rode the city bus and then walked ten blocks to ride the cable car to Annalee's apartment, all this time with baby Toby fast asleep in my arms, not a cry out of him as I managed bus fare and curious women asking about my "baby". I put them off, all except one friendly looking lady. I uncovered "baby" just a peek, with fingers to my lips! She understood and said not a word.

Years later when Toby came to live with me he was an elderly tom cat. I'm sure he missed his Annalee, but we soon became good friends and enjoyed getting to know and love one another. The cat house has been deserted for several years since Toby went to cat heaven.

RUTH AND TOBY

Chapter 2
LADY'S GIFT TO RUTH

I was enjoying a beautiful, sunny Saturday morning in my back yard and had just picked a bouquet of yellow daisies to sit on my dining room table when I thought I heard a faint "meow" –no- I must have imagined it – yes – it was a very pretty gray cat with white patches, meowing for my attention. He looked half-starved and against my better judgment I offered him a bowl of food. Of course he stayed; however, it seems "he" turned out to be a very pregnant "she". I named her Lady.

Lady seemed so happy to be with me, but then one day she disappeared; I was so upset, I had come to enjoy her company and I missed her. Had she met with a disaster, maybe hit by a car, or had she found a new home?

A week or so later as I was raking the yard early one morning, Lady returned bringing me a gift, a tiny blue-gray kitten that she carried in her mouth and dropped at my feet. I named the baby Bluey because Annalee had a cat named Bluey when she was a little girl. For several days she left for a few hours each day, then would come back to nurse her baby. It was more than a week later, on a Sunday afternoon, when she appeared carrying another baby, a tiny black kitten. Since it was Sunday, Sunnie seemed a good name for Bluey's little brother. Next day she came bringing, of course, Monnie. Monnie was also black but with a white bib and little white feet. On Tuesday, Lady presented me with the last of her litter, Tuessie. I believe Lady must have been testing me to see how well I would take care of the first baby that she dropped at my feet before she trusted me with the rest of her family. It must have been quite a feat for her to carry her four babies in her mouth, one at a time, from their birthplace to my back yard.

A GIFT FOR RUTH

DINNER TIME

NAP TIME

Chapter 3
A GOOD MOMMY

Lady is such a good mommy; it is heartwarming how she loves her babies. I firmly believe she has never been cross with any of them, She holds them down, one at a time, and cleans them from head to toe. She takes special care to clean their ears, inside and out.

I have been trying to teach lady not to bother the birds. Annalee and I had Toby trained to "live and let live", but my Lady lived another life before she came here; however, she does not seem to take me for granted, and wants to cooperate in every way. Whenever I have to correct her she seems hurt and humiliated, something unusual for cats. I am fascinated by her intelligence and how she is trying to teach her babies to be good. They are so cute and so active and all over the place! In their play I never hear growling or cries. They bite – they bite me too—but it is always a playful bite. The thing I must be careful of is their nails, as they are extremely sharp and long and they hang on. The kittens are all naughty about climbing up on the screen door when they want indoors. So far they have managed to get down from all the high places, but I fear the day will come when they can't or won't jump down.

I believe my cat family came to me because we needed each other- of course, the babies couldn't help themselves. Their mother brought them to me! I say I'm taking it easy these days! That word "easy" I must change to "as easy as possible" with a feline family of five to care for.

Lady tries to coax me to sit down so that she can jump upon my lap for the stroking and petting she enjoys so much. For some reason, and I don't understand why, she whines a lot when she and I are alone. She doesn't do that when she is with her babies. Perhaps she is trying to tell me that it is time for me to take all five of them to the vet for their shots.

Though I keep telling myself, "I cannot keep this family of cats", how can I help myself? They are darling babies, just little puff balls! I don't know if I could ever give any of them away. Perhaps I shouldn't have adopted Lady and her babies, but I tell myself that my maternal instinct forced me into it, or it could be that I was influenced by "All CREATURES GREAT and SMALL", a book that I have been reading. I had thought that I would never, never assume the responsibility of raising cats again, but here I am with my adopted feline family —or did they adopt me?

PROUD MOMMY

Chapter 4
KITTY CAPERS

Grocery day is work for me. I carry in cans and cans of cat food and milk. Mother and babies all love milk; I give it to them at noon and they lick the platter clean. I always experience a thrill when I come home from shopping and find my cat family so happy to see me; of course they always peek at me from behind a protective tree trunk or from behind a mass of leaves to determine when it is safe to come out. When I came home yesterday, Jim the gardener was here but not one cat was visible. When Jim left, I could see bright little eyes peeking out from their hiding places. When I called them they all came running.

I've run out of food that Lady likes, so I've been feeding her canned tuna and chicken. She doesn't like dry cat food. I wonder if she would like raw hamburger? I will buy some next time I go grocery shopping and feed it to her very sparingly, as it might not be good for her. Her babies like everything in sight. They devour their cat food, then lie down with Mother and begin working, each on their favorite faucet. She seems to love it and so do they. They are all getting fat, except Tuesse, she is scrawny and looks just like her mother. There is something about Lady's build; she is very long and almost sway-back, as are tigers and leopards.

This morning I gave each of my babies a brushing with their new brush. They are becoming less afraid of me and seem to love it. They all have beautiful eyes, very expressive. Little Monnie's eyes are deep blue and she has a very interesting face, as if she had been "made up" for a show or a clown act. My kittens are all so different in both looks and personalities that I can't help but wonder how many fathers they had! I know now that I can't part with any of them willingly. A teenager wanted little Bluey as a birthday gift for his sister and I refused. I was afraid he might be mistreated. I couldn't let him go!

It is chilly and very cold outside. My cat family prefers to be indoors on days like this. They are all full of mischief and race from room to room, where they upset, spill, and topsy-turvy everything in their way.

One day I looked all over the house for Bluey but he was nowhere to be found. Mother cat found him and I suspect she knew all-along that he was sound asleep under the telephone stand in the kitchen. Lady is now on my lap and being very possessive of my attention. I had my left arm resting around her and she got the idea that my arm needed a washing. I do believe she pulled hair out with her tongue. She would throw her head back and up and look intently at me. When I count my blessings, I include my feline family. I think that I couldn't live here alone without them. Whatever did I do before they came to live with me?

Tuessie had sneaked into the kitchen one evening as I was preparing my dinner. I accidently stepped on her poor little tail; she yowled so loudly that the rafters shook! Any time I accidently hurt her, she thinks I do it on purpose. She was still upset with me the next day. She seems to be the only member of her cat family who holds a grudge for so long. My cleaning lady will be here tomorrow and I will ask her to take Tuessie to the vet with her sore tail—that is if Tuessie can be found! Life is sometimes a lot of "ifs. Poor Tuessie's tail; it must be so sore and she must be so ashamed of how it looks—maybe I can buy a cat wig and glue it on her tail!

Bluey, the adventurous one, squeezed through a crack in the door while his brothers and sisters were hungrily devouring their dinner in the back yard. Minutes later, Bluey was nowhere to be seen in the house, although I could hear sounds coming from somewhere. I had closed bedroom and bathroom doors in an attempt to trap him and keep him from racing from room to room with me in hot pursuit. I followed the sounds I heard, opened the bedroom door and there he was on the dresser--admiring himself in the mirror. What a charmer! He walked across the dresser toward me so I could pick him up. He was so sweet and adorable that I couldn't say a cross word to him. You see, it was really my fault! A few days earlier I had carried him to the various mirrors so that he could see himself. I suppose he wanted to try it alone. They are all so special and with their own personalities. It would be so lonesome without them! Sometimes their capers play me out and I am thankful when their little bellies are full to bulging and they have found cozy places for a few hours of sleep. It has taken me awhile to "outsmart" them, to learn how to cope with them, and they are learning to behave a bit better.

Mother cat is nursing her babies now and all is quiet. I've been putting them out at night and letting them indoors in the early morning. My reasoning is that this way I get a full night's sleep, however, now that Sunnie has learned to climb to the top of the screen door and cry for help getting down, he is likely to try it at night! I'm sure he could back down, but it is so much easier to cry for me to help.

You should see Lady trying to avoid her children when they chase after her bosoms! She takes refuge by begging to come in the front door. She will have surgery next week. I'm fretting, as I know she will be terribly upset and worried. Her babies can manage alone, but she is so protective of them. I know she will put up a big fight and grieve. I'll let her come indoors and stay overnight with me.

LADY

Chapter 5

OCCI

My vet believes that there is a "cat nurse" helping those who are homeless and hungry find shelter and food. That must be how Occi came to me. She was all but "done in" when she came to my door; she was starved, poor baby, and looked as though she must have traveled many miles. There was a story in our local paper about a new breed of cats called "Occicats", originating from the wild ocelot. That was the reason for my naming our newcomer Occi.

My Occi has deep stripes or bands on her legs. She has so many marks of the wild animal along with the sweet traits of the domesticated. Her ears have little hairs sticking straight up out of them like little wigwams with smoke coming out of the peaks. She is so intelligent, just don't pet her for too long. "Enuf is enuf", she says, and with a low rumbling under her ribs you will get a bite or a scratch. She can love one moment, and the wild comes out before you expect it.

I have noticed Occi taking up food with her right paw and eating from it. I've never seen an animal do this, except squirrels and raccoons. This must be caused by a gene from her ocelot ancestry, as it is not a domesticated cat characteristic.

I've been wasting my time trying to discipline Occi—just doesn't work and I may as well give up! She is so mean to her adopted sisters, Monnie and Tuessie, and I am unable to correct her! She is surely full of some wild blood. Although she is very smart, she gets ornery spells and would just as soon tear into me, with her long claws, as another animal. She slaps my hands for doing something she doesn't approve of. She always uses her left paw for disciplining me, but takes up her food with her right paw.

Occi loves to watch TV, especially the animal shows. She used to think that the animals on TV were real and would put her paws on the screen as if she wanted to join in the race or whatever was going on, but she soon learned they were only pictures to be watched, not touched. She is an expert at unplugging appliances, wherever an appliance is plugged into a wall socket.

Occi isn't all cat, you know. She loves to sit in the high chair and eat. She is very dainty about picking her food up with her paw and putting it in her mouth, and then she cleans her "hands" very well, licking between her "fingers". I should make a little bib for her to wear when she sits in her high chair and eats from her bowl.

My teenagers all love to play games. Occi runs from another room, jumps onto a throw rug, slides across the room and ends up stopped by a chair, in a heap or a pile. She loves playing this game and grins from ear to ear. Another of her favorites is playing "pick up". She climbs up on the dining room table and begins scattering papers until she finds a pencil or pen. She then takes her paw and "swish—swish" this way and that and there go my precious letters onto the floor. Nothing lost, nothing eliminated—but can hear her saying, "Now it is your job, your duty, to pick up your papers and put them in order!" Or, she sits in my lap when I write and tries to take the pen from me with her little paws and she usually wins the battle. You see, she thinks all the pens and pencils belong to her and that they are her toys; she loves batting them around on the floor and chasing them. She takes them apart, plays with the parts and then hides them. She does let me use my pens part of the time, if I can find them.

OCCI WITH TOY

OCCI

Chapter 6
LIL BOY BLUE

I have two friends living across the street from me, the "Two Pauls". They are so good to me always bringing me treats, such as a container of noodle soup or some other food they have heard me say that I like. Their pet, a beautiful, blue-gray, male cat, often followed them to my house where he met and made friends with my feline family. One day he decided to stay and has made no effort to return home. He sits in my yard and watches his owners across the street but does not venture out of my yard. He fits in with my cats and seems to be happy with us. Perhaps he gets more attention here as both of the Pauls work all day.

I have named him Lil Boy Blue. At this moment he is helping me write and planting kisses on my face.   I will take the hint, stop writing and pay more attention to him. I think that both Occi and Lil Boy Blue had to give up their mothers too soon and this is why they think of me as their mother. Monnie and Tuessie got to be weaned by their mother and don't require all the additional love from me.

Lil Boy Blue is giving me such a loving that I almost need to protect myself! He love-bites bits of my chin, my nose and big slices of my cheek. He is the only cat that has ever tried to make love to me so exuberantly. He must be Italian, you know, his daddy, Paul, is Italian.

Lil Boy Blue is a prime example of unusual behavior: when indoors he will make a flying leap from the china closet to the table, to the top of the refrigerator, and back to the china closet. I finally capture him, and "whish" out of doors he goes. Recently, I was watering in the back yard when an object came from the back of me and sailed over my head! It was Lil Boy Blue! He amazes me that he can jump so high and sail for such a long distance. After his sailing experience, he fell asleep in a box on the patio with a rug in it and I covered him with an old towel. Lil Boy Blue demonstrates his gentlemanly nature and always backs away from food until his brothers and sisters have been served, and then he eats only from his bowl. Monnie, the fat one, will eat from any bowl at any time.

LIL BOY BLUE FLYING

Chapter 7
PUDDY

Puddy, my little cat visitor, lives in a house on the hilltop behind my house. He comes to visit at dinnertime almost every day. I wish I could adopt him. He is a beautiful white Persian and has such an unusual face with all of his features to the front. His nose is very short, like a piece of putty stuck on his face. His eyes are big and round and he looks as if he is wearing eyeliner. His mouth is up front where you can see it. A cat's mouth should be back under his face, but not Puddy: his mouth is up front, just like mine. He seems almost more human than animal! He has a long, bushy mustache—like a country bumpkin's long, unkempt mustache.

My cats begin looking for Puddy to come down the hill about the same time every day. Occi is the official hostess when Puddy comes to visit. She brings him into the house for his tuna fish meal and then takes him part way home. I call Puddy's mommy to assure that he gets home OK. She tells me that she watches for him. I love that little fellow and I stop everything when he comes to visit. He has such a dear, sweet face and a little laughing mouth. Puddy's mommy has a new baby and I fear that her Puddy has been neglected. He has had a dirty face and matted hair and has been refusing to come in the house as if he was ashamed of his appearance. When he came to visit last night, however, he walked right into the kitchen, wiggling and grinning from ear to ear. He had been bathed, had a haircut, and seemed so very proud of himself. When Puddy comes down and I am not in the yard, he comes to the kitchen door and calls me in his cute little, half cat, half human voice. He is such a beautiful cat and certainly makes himself the center of attention. He is always hungry and always eager to explore. His eyes are green, but sometimes they look blue more like human eyes because they are so expressive. His highness has learned to enjoy roast chicken as well as tuna and goes after either with great gusto.

RUTH AND PUDDY

Chapter 8
TEENAGERS

My cats are in the feistiest, naughtiest, most playful and active stage of their young lives. Although they are teenagers, they still like to burrow into their mommy's shaved, white belly and find their own special faucet. She allows it for a few minutes and actually seems to enjoy it.

The teenagers love being indoors and somehow they do manage to sneak in—then just try to get them out! They are like greased lightning! Their mommy gets upset because they are so unruly, but Lady is a very loving and tolerant mommy. It always amazes me how she seems to understand what I am saying to her. I must admit, I have been doing a lot of complaining to her lately about her naughty kids! These domesticated, teenage felines are constantly figuring out ways to outsmart me. I can't keep up with them; they sneak indoors and race from room to room like wild animals. They roll up rugs, run across beds, and just as I think I can get my hands on them, they are gone like a flash. I finally got all of them out, except Sunnie. I was just too bushed to continue the game of "chase"; I gave up, rested and read the Sunday paper. When I awakened from a little nap to look for Sunnie, he was sound asleep on a folded, black afghan on the back of my recliner, not showing a sign of remembering what a little demon he had been just an hour earlier.

My cats are so special in so many ways, in both their looks and their personalities. Last night I invited Lady indoors to watch TV with me. She came in and after inspecting the living room, seemed to enjoy sitting on my lap and my stroking her silky fur (it feels just like real silk). In about fifteen minutes she jumped down from my lap and went to the dining room where she stood by the window, watching her family roughhouse and tumble. I opened the door for her to go out and they seemed so happy to be together. They are such a happy animal family! They are all so beautifully colored and they seem so like people with almost human emotions. Lady loves her family so much and takes wonderful care of them. In all their play together, there is never an outcry. They toss and tumble and they bite, but it is all in the spirit of play. I am learning that cats are very perceptive. They do a good job of reading between the lines and knowing what is on a human's mind. All of my cats know their names and respond (if they choose to do so) when I call them. I talk to them so much and they know some things I say, if not the actual words, then perhaps the voice inflection, I use mainly short sentences and those that imply action on either their part or mine.

I spend many hours watching my feline teenagers at play in the back yard. They climb trees and they climb over fences out of and back into our yard. One day I tied two long ribbons to the acacia tree branch for a little "kitty fun". As little Monnie was batting them or trying to but usually falling on her fanny, I noticed that the strands of ribbon were getting shorter and shorter. I looked up and saw a squirrel sitting on the branch, poking the ribbon into his mouth as fast as he could. I started to rush over to retrieve the ribbon but squirrel made one last pull and quickly stuffed the last of the ribbon into his mouth. I worried that he would suffocate before he could free himself from that ribbon! There is never a dull moment around here! Another day I was watching Sunnie trying to get his head into my watering can to get a drink of water; when that didn't work he cupped his paw and drank from his "hand". The water apparently tasted pretty good so he repeated the process. When I was a little girl my dad taught me to drink from the Medicine Creek, running through our farm in Nebraska, using my hands in the same way.

Possibly one should not get so much joy, and feel such closeness to a dear little animal. I imagine it is partly because I live alone except for my cat family. I love and seem to need these creatures. Annalee used to be this way with her animals. We both have always needed someone to love and someone to love us. I'm sure she would have approved of my feline family. This family of mine is so very, very special!

RUTH IN BACK YARD SWING

PLAY TIME

BLUEY CHASING HER TAIL

Chapter 9
FAMILY OF SEVEN AND MORE

My blessed babies, what would my life be without them? They really are no longer babies. They have changed over the years. Occi has gotten fat and her fur is very thick and long. She still has her feisty but loving disposition.

Boy Blue has grown, but not fat. He has characteristics that I've not before seen in a cat. He is so jealous of Occi that it is upsetting our way of life! Having her in his home and sitting on his mommy's lap has turned the sweet mannered little boy into a beast when he is around Occi. If Occi isn't near, he curls up in my favorite dining room chair and I use a substitute. He awakens from time to time, climbs onto my lap and covers my face with kisses. He so easily turns from "mighty warrior" to a forceful, eager lover—just like all males. Boy Blue has also started the war game of fighting the throw rugs by the front door. When he has the "enemy" subdued, he curls up beside the "hill" he has formed and falls asleep. One day one of his sisters had him wrapped up in a throw rug, like a "pig in a blanket". She was pouncing on him and rolling him over and over. It was so clever of them, but also a windfall for me. I carried him, blanket and all, to the door—released him—and their fun was over. Just having one cat in the house at a time is such a different story, each one is a little angel!

Sunnie is the quiet one; he loves to sit in my warm lap where he can cuddle with me. One look into those bright, beautiful eyes and I melt! However, Sunnie has been grounded from the house for a few days because he has been mean to his little sister, Tuessie.

Little Tuessie is small and aggressive, a little darling. Tuessie had hidden by the side of my chair in the living room, early this evening, so she could jump upon my lap when I sat down to watch TV—before anyone else beat her to it. She had simply grown tired of having to pile in with one of her siblings for a snooze on that soft warm lap.

Monnie is shy—a bit afraid—but overcoming her fears. She may be the prettiest of Lady's babies. Sunnie is black with white paws and he seems to be his mommy's favorite. Bluey is the leader, so beautiful and so proper.

I'm sitting at the kitchen table and Bluey is on the table trying to climb upon my lap and demanding my attention. He is singing me a sweet "song" and I am trying to teach him that the kitchen table in a "no-no". He sits here supervising my writing. I don't know where his brothers and sisters are, but I suspect that they are visiting our neighbors as I saw two of them jump over the fence into our neighbor's yard; so far they have always returned home, but I do worry about them. I wish I could get our feline family to stay in our yard and away from danger, but that isn't cat nature. Their thinking is that the world belongs to all who claim it. These kids also love to come indoors. They race and frolic and dare me to catch them, the little imps!

All my cats have very "human like" personality traits. They have one personality when they are alone with me and another when a brother or sister comes along. Occi is such an intelligent cat. I've seen it many times. She understands much that I say to her and answers in her own way, which I can't fail to interpret or understand. At night when I say "It's time for bed" Occi heads for the living room and beds down on some pillows. Most animals that are loved become smart and understanding and show unconditional love for their owners.

CUDDLING KITTENS

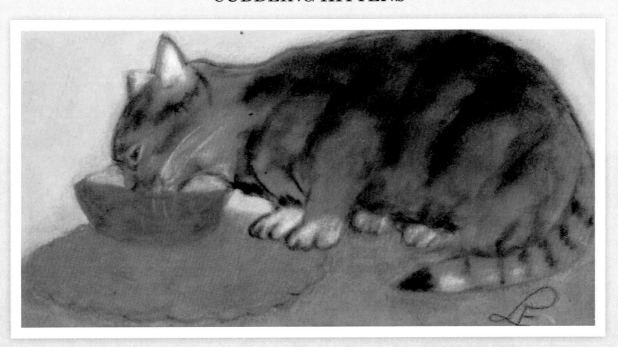

DINNER TIME

Chapter 10
KITTY LOVE

Monnie and Tuessie were cuddling this morning, cheek to cheek, and arms holding each other. I've never seen cats so affectionate. Monnie loved Tuessie with every lick of her little tongue, She licked and licked over her sister's neck, mouth, eyes and ears, then tired and relaxed. Little sister then began returning the love and affection. After their baths, they cuddled up on a pillow and there they stayed for hours. It was so dear of them and showed how much they must love one another. There is a picture on one of my calendars of one cat grooming another (could be my Monnie and Tuessie) and the quote, "You scratch my ears and when you are through I may do something nice for you"—but you mustn't count on that, 'cause after all, I am a cat".

A few days later, I saw Bluey and his sister, Tuessie on the roof of the patio—making love! They were both stretched out, full length, and Bluey had arms around his sister caressing and loving her. She had her eyes closed and the happiest look on her face! Me thinks, time for a trip to the vet. I have a great big dread of taking my cats to the vet for surgery.

A male cat has been visiting our yard lately, attempting to interest our girl cats. Boy Blue and this stranger have been at war. The girls take to the patio roof and stay there as long as it takes Boy Blue to chase the intruder away. This has given Boy Blue courage to challenge others passing by. Well, he was giving his usual war cry, and I decided to help him out with a cry from the open kitchen door: "You go away, leave our little girls alone". The stranger didn't move, so I opened the door wider and looked into a pair of beautiful green eyes and a sleek black body. It was our Sunnie! It was no wonder he wouldn't go away, for this was his home too. His cat mommy had brought him as a baby to this mommy—me—and I had loved him and named him Sunnie. I'll never know why he left me to go live with a neighbor, but he did. He still came to see us whenever he wished to and I have always put food out for him. Boy Blue quit yelling at Sunnie as soon as he saw it was OK with me for him to be in our yard. You know, cats are much smarter than we realize they are. Sunnie doesn't forget us but he must have a good home as he is very beautiful, clean, and looks well fed. This one time was the only time that he seemed to be hungry—I'm glad he knew where to come. I hoped that Boy Blue wouldn't forget who Sunnie was the next time he came to visit. It was only days later when Sunnie returned and I heard Boy Blue's war cry. I rushed out, trying to placate them but neither gave in; they both continued glaring and daring with vicious growls, but they could hardly go to battle with me between them! Sunnie is so pretty, but he makes terrible faces when his temper flares.

That was the last time I saw Sunnie. My neighbor, Mrs. Jones, came over the next morning to tell me that Sunnie had been hit by a car and killed. I had been trying to teach Boy Blue to consider Sunnie as one of our feline family and not to fight him, but, being the only male in the family, I'm sure Boy Blue was just being protective of his females.

Chapter 11

EARTHQUAKE

I had let Bluey inside, but then regretted it as he didn't seem to be his usual placid self. He did settle in the green chair in the living room, but just couldn't seem to relax. He started scratching and fighting the back of the chair. I scolded him and he jumped down. I had moved to my usual chair at the kitchen table when all of a sudden he jumped onto my shoulders, his left leg straddling my left shoulder, his right leg on my right shoulder, his belly against my head and began digging his claws into my hair. I toppled him over. Then, just a few minutes later, Tuessie tried to climb onto my shoulders. I believe they may have felt the earthquake that hit Oakland at that exact time. This was the only time that I had been near any of my cats during earthquake activity. I have heard that cows, horses and even caged birds are uneasy and restless when there are earthquakes.

Not long after the earthquake, Bluey disappeared. I hope he found a new home but I fear he may have met the same fate as his brother, Sunnie, his sister, Monnie, and perhaps his mother. I am giving Tuessie extra love and attention these days, as I know she grieves for her sister, Monnie, who helped her so much with her grooming. She washed Tuessie's ears and her head and all difficult places to reach. Tuessie spends much of her time sitting on my lap, as she is doing now.

Monnie was unhappy and didn't seem to fit in with the other cats. They picked on her, all except Tuessie. Monnie loved her little sister, Tuessie, and was fond of me, but she wouldn't mind me. I grieve for her and wonder if her death was a suicide! She was hit by a car. I think maybe she may have been trying to leave home and did this on purpose.

I don't recall ever fretting so over the other cats I have had. Perhaps because they came to me as kittens with no mother cat to interfere. Just when Lady's family became teenagers and needed a lot of discipline she disappeared. Sometimes cats find new homes or maybe Lady just needed a rest from four very demanding children, or perhaps she went in search of a male to start a new family. I miss her.

Now I have just Occi, Boy Blue, Tuessie and our visitor, Puddy. They fill my days with love, adventure and the feeling of being needed. I am so lucky to have them!

THE PLAYFUL ONE

Chapter 12
GOODBYES

One must always begin a journal entry with a bit of cheer, so I shall. It is a nice warm day, which we have all been asking for. I feel good today—beautiful sunshine and all is well with the world.

One thing that does bug me—forgive me for complaining (one more time and this journal hits the waste basket). I should be outside watering my plants, but I'm not walking well today, a good reason to put a person in "tatters and shreds". I want so much to have a tidy, well-kept home, but I am finding it difficult to take care of my house and of my cat family. Though I have tried keeping my cats outside, I get lonely and I feel like a mean old mommy living alone in comfort, while their little bodies are shivering with the cold.

My little companions have been very close to me lately, showing me a lot of love. They seem to know when all is not well. I do get so tired these days, from the top of my head to the tip of my toes. Many times my mind goes on vacation and I'm not always sure when or if it is coming back. But life goes on and we must learn to cope in the best way we can—turn our thoughts to other things.

I am so happy to be alive and enjoying my feline family. Boy Blue is taking my mind off my problems. He has jumped onto my lap and is biting on the end of my pen. He has won this round! I'll admit, I am in his chair and he is telling me it is time to go to bed. My cats are all so very intelligent. I wonder, maybe I am the one who is not so bright, the really dumb "animal".

These days I find myself wondering who will be the first to say goodbye, me or my cats. As I approach my ninety fourth birthday, I am the only one left in my immediate family. I thank God every day for my health and for my faithful feline companions, who over the years have helped me laugh and smile and appreciate all life has to offer.

RUTH AND LADY

EPILOGUE

With the help of a wonderful, live-in caretaker, named Andrea, Ruth was able to stay in her own home and enjoy her feline companions for several more years. She left us at age ninety-eight. Tuessie, Boy Blue and Occi found good homes, but I am sure they missed their Ruth.

This is a story of unconditional love of animals for their humans. The adage, "A house is not a home without a pet" is so true. Caring for a pet teaches children responsibility and gives a sense of being loved and needed. Unconditional love is shown when a puppy gives his boy or girl kisses on the cheek or a kitty curls up in their lap and purrs. When the love children give their pets is given back to them it enhances their self-esteem. Pets supply a nurturing quality by means of the affection and attention they show for their humans.

The unconditional love of an animal for their human also makes life more meaningful and less lonely for those of us in the winter years of our lives by giving us companionship, love, a feeling of being needed, and a sense of security and protection. Statistics tell us that the elderly live longer, happier lives when they have a pet.

Love is the most important health attribute we have and pets are one of nature's best sources of love. Pets help us unwind; they can make us laugh and divert our mind away from troubles. Several recent studies have shown that having a pet to love can aid in relaxation, promote good health and extend one's life.

According to recent studies, pets seem to have an amazing positive impact on stress, cholesterol levels and blood pressure. Animals have always played an important part in the story of my life. My parents realized the importance of pets in their children's lives as a way of teaching them responsibility and appreciation for the love shared between them and their pets.

The photos my mother took of my brother, Harold, (ca 1920) with his Collie, Carlos, and of me and my cat, Bluey, (ca 1925), photos and copies of paintings that I have done over the years of my children, grandchildren and great grandchildren with their pets help tell the story of the love animals feel for their humans.

A recent article in AARP MAGAZINE, says in part: "Dogs confer a host of wellness benefits, especially to kids and older people. People with dogs sleep better, weigh less and get more exercise than their dog-free peers. Having a dog imparts lessons about love and friendship and teaches one how to be a better person."

People with pets are less lonely and enjoy better self-esteem than non-pet owners, a Miami University study shows. "Pets reduce cortisol, a stress hormone, while boosting oxytocin, the same pain-easing, mood-lifting chemical you experience when you are in love," explains psychologist Denee Jordon. And that happy feeling delivers another benefit: It strengthens your resistance to germs!

According to the American Heart Association, living with a pet drops your risk of heart disease as much as 30%! A top reason: Animal companions reduce dangerous blood pressure spikes by 23%, according to research done at the State University of New York at Buffalo. Pet owners are less likely to be overweight, reveals a study at the Berkeley University of California, The reason is because they move more often! In fact, a different study found that dog owners walk twice as much every day as non-dog owners.

Bluey was my first pet and she must have loved me very much to have put up with me carrying her upside down!

POOR CAT

My first dog was Snooky, a tiny Rat Terrier that I taught to jump through a hoop and to sit in my doll's high chair. By the time I was a first grader, my dog Tricksie, a "Heinz Variety," walked the mile and a half to school with me each morning and would be waiting for me at four o'clock, when school was dismissed, to walk me safely home. One day on his way to school to pick me up he was hit by a car and killed. I cried for days!

Then there was Snoopy Pedro, a stray that I brought home from school, where someone had ditched him. I talked our teacher, Mrs. Connell, into letting him stay in the school room until I could take him home with me. He was no doubt hungry and kept sniffing at our Karo syrup lunch buckets. Mrs. Connell named him Snoopy Pedro. We soon discovered that Snoopy Pedro had the bad habit of sucking eggs! My dad and I tried loading an egg with red pepper, but it didn't discourage him. (He must have been part Chihuahua!). It was difficult for me to part with Snoopy, but I could understand why my dad couldn't let me keep him. Eggs were an important commodity to help pay for our groceries during the "dirty thirties". Snoopy found a new home where there were no eggs to suck.

My oldest brother, Harold, had a pet dog, a Collie named Carlos. This painting reveals the love Carlos felt for his boy!

CARLOS AND HIS BOY

Just as there were always pets in my childhood home, my family of five children also had many pets, including dogs, cats, fish, a rabbit and a turtle to share their love and to teach them responsibility. Over a span of many years I have done many paintings of my children, grandchildren and great grandchildren with their pets and have included them in this story. My oldest daughter, Sharllyn, was a toddler when Spotty, an Alaskan Husky and Fox Terrier mix breed, came to live with us and stayed for thirteen years. Spotty's mother was a show dog. The puppy was only a few days old and suffering from heat exposure when she was given to us by a lady at the circus with the comment, "Maybe you can keep her alive." Sharllyn helped feed her with a doll baby bottle and nipple and they bonded. We lived along a very busy street and didn't have a fenced in back yard. When Sharllyn ventured beyond the sidewalk, Spotty grabbed her by the seat of the pants and brought her back within the safety zone.

SHARLLYN AND SPOTTY

Spotty was a few years old and Sharllyn had a little sister, Carolyn, when a beautiful, white Persian cat joined our family. The girls had been feeding her in a shed back of our house, but hadn't told me what they were doing. One day she followed them to the house and with her baby blue eyes pleaded with me to please give her a home. She was obviously very, very pregnant and needed a home for herself and her babies. Both girls joined in the plea, "Please Mommy, can we keep her?" We named her Snowball. A few days later, she found a nest for three fluffy little "snowballs" in the girls' pajama drawer.

Neutering a pet was not as popular in those days as it is today. We always sold our puppies and kittens and found good homes for them. My belief was that when some money was invested, the pet was given a better home.

One time Spotty mated with an Alaskan Husky and one of her puppies was large, like a Husky. Who should answer the ad "Puppies for sale" but a former boyfriend of mine, Gaylord, who had served in World War Two and came home a hero and a paraplegic. His dog, Spotty's puppy, became a much loved companion and pulled him around the house in his wheelchair.

Spotty and Snowball had become good friends over the years when both had litters of babies at the same time. Snowball's kittens were only a few days old when she disappeared, not to return. Spotty adopted those three baby kittens, nursing and caring for them along with her own babies.

I am the mother of five children, with a span of twenty one years between the birthdays of my oldest and my youngest. We always had pets and the pets always became part of our family.

When my Beckie Jo and my Michael were growing up we had a Siamese cat named Candy (because she always stole Beckie's candy) and a male Siamese, named Kitty Kim. They parented several litters of kittens. When the first litter was born, I tried to keep them separated, thinking that the male might hurt the kittens. I was so mistaken! Kitty Kim cried and begged until I relented and let him join his family. From that day on Daddy Kitty Kim was the caretaker. He sat with the babies, washed them from head to toe and loved them. Candy, the proud, sophisticated one, went to their nest in the basement only long enough to feed them. She would much rather be upstairs, sitting very prim and proper! One day I found her on the kitchen counter with the cupboard door open where I kept my silver tea set. There she sat, using the tea pot as a mirror to groom herself! Candy was a one- person cat. She really didn't like anyone except Beckie. Kitty Kim, on the other hand, was very cross-eyed and very loving and lovable, just a big teddy bear. Beckie, who is now a grandmother, always has and still does love her Siamese cats.

CANDY AND KITTY KIMS' BABIES

My oldest son, Michael, had a room filled with aquariums for his collection of fish—many different kinds, from Gold Fish to Piranhas. He also had a pet turtle, named "Big Mama", who was one of our most interesting pets. Zak was the name of his German Shepherd dog who followed him to college. Michael's oldest grandson, Gannon, and his two younger brothers now have an aquarium of fish and two pet dogs, but so far they don't have a turtle!

Michael and I were on our way home to North Dakota from Nebraska when Michael spied a large Western Painted Turtle sauntering down the middle of highway 183. We stopped the car to keep from hitting it. Michael wanted to give it a home and of course Mom said, "Yes, you may take her home with us." We christened her "Big Mama." She adapted to life at 1100 N. First Street very quickly, even learning to use the pet door like our dogs and cats did. She would mosey down the sidewalk in front of our house and then come back in the house through the pet door. Her favorite sleeping spot was on a warm cushion back of our black and white television in the basement recreation room.

BOY AND TURTLE

My youngest child, Robert Allen, was just a toddler when I painted "Bobby and Kitty Kim". There was no doubt that it was "unconditional love" that Kitty Kim showed for Bobby when he pulled the poor cat around by his tail and sat on him. Bobby's first dog was Wendy, a Schnauzer puppy who joined our family. She had just had her ears cropped when she arrived by plane from a kennel in Minneapolis. At the time Bobby had an infection in one of his finger nails and his hand was bandaged. I changed the bandage and soaked his finger several times a day keeping the gauze, medication and scissors on a tray for convenience. We had been home with our new puppy for only a few hours when I found Bobby on the bed with Wendy—tray close by—scissors in hand—ready to change Wendy's bandage!

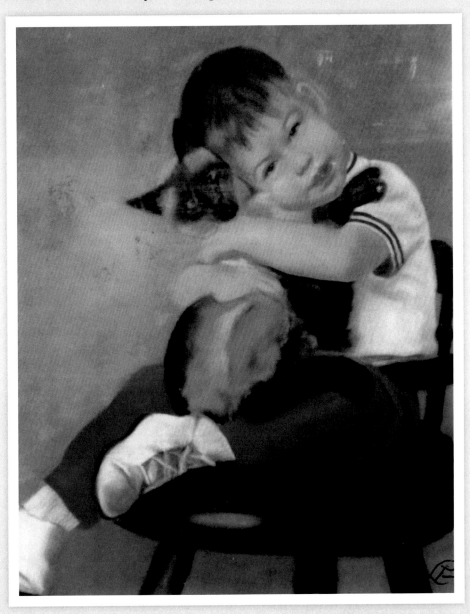

BOBBY AND KITTY KIM

Kiki was Bobby's cat, a "Heinz Variety" and very intelligent. She would go out the pet door to the back yard; to get back indoors, she would climb onto the milk box so that she could reach and ring the doorbell (in those days milk was delivered to a box at our doorstep in one-quart glass bottles). Another user of our pet door was Herman, a loveable big black rabbit that we found at a yard sale.

BOBBY AND KIKI

Bobby had a new playmate when a beautiful, playful, white German Shepherd joined our household. We named him Czar. Czar's mother was a guard dog. I was convinced that if Czar was given plenty of love, he would not grow up displaying his mother's genes. Bobby built a Lincoln Log fort for him.

PUPPY CZAR

Czar was a faithful companion and our protector for more than thirteen years. Visitors didn't get past the front door until I said, "It's O.K., Czar." When a carpet installer began tearing out old carpeting in the family room, Czar, very gently took the man's hand in his mouth and waited for me to say, "It's O.K., Czar " before letting go. In the same way he kept my cleaning lady's little, three year old daughter from pulling her baby sister off the bed by gently holding her hand in his mouth until I came to the baby's rescue.

Czar would jump over our five-foot, backyard redwood fence and walk to a nearby shopping center to find my car when I went shopping, then back home and over the fence. He would be waiting at the door to greet me when I came home with my arms full of groceries. I would not have known this had my neighbors not seen it happen, time and time again.

After dinner was playtime. When Czar needed a new tennis ball he took my hand in his mouth and led me to the basement. He stopped in the laundry room and pointed his head to a shelf where I kept a box of tennis balls.

Czar saw me through some rough times in my life during the years he took care of me. He licked many a tear from my cheek. No, Czar couldn't talk, but he understood and always seemed to find a way to get his message across. Even though Czar lived a long life, losing him was extremely painful for me. I cried myself to sleep many nights. At the time I lost Czar, Bobby had a cat named Kitty, another Siamese that seemed to be a one-person cat. She slept with Bobby. However, when I lost my Czar, Kitty left Bobby's room and came to sleep with me, purring and cuddling up to me. She seemed to know that I was hurting and needed her love. When I brought another dog to be with me, she went back to Bobby's room.

CZAR

Tina, a West Highland Terrier, had some big shoes to fill when she came to us over a year after we had lost Czar, but she tried so hard.

My husband, Bob, was suffering from dementia. She sat on his lap for hours at a time to be petted. He asked, "Why doesn't she purr?" "Because she isn't a cat," I answered, "she is a dog."

Tina was in the car with me when I was in the car accident that changed my life. My cousin, Winona, took care of her during my six weeks of hospitalization. She brought Tina to visit me often and their visits always brightened my day. Tina was a natural at cheering the sick and elderly as I had often taken her to the nursing home where my uncle was living and many of the residents looked forward to her visits.

TINA

My paintings and photographs portray the love of my grandchildren for their pets. Studies have revealed that children who had a dog or cat as a pet before they were a year old had 31% fewer respiratory infections and 44% lower ear infections.

Researchers say that when kids read aloud to a pet their reading skills improve up to 12% in just 10 weeks. Why? Pets are non-judgmental and make encouraging listeners.

Sharllyn's daughter, Cindy, always loved horses. She started cleaning stables and grooming horses at a very early age in exchange for riding lessons. Her first horse was J. P. (Just Perfect)

JUST PERFECT

Throughout her teen-age and early adult years Cindy and "Talk Of The Town" participated in 'Hunter's Jumping Class" competition. She is dressed in Equestrian attire.

IN COMPETITION

TALK OF THE TOWN

After Cindy married and had children, Tyler, Jacob and Tristan, there were always pets – cats, dogs, hamsters, and birds, including a parrot. Tyler and his dog, Aspen, a Jack Russell, are portrayed in my painting titled "Love In A Heartbeat". As a teen-ager Tyler had a Dachsund named Phoebe. Tyler was Phoebe's boy. When Tyler was ill and confined to bed, Phoebe stole food from the kitchen and brought it to Tyler.

LOVE IN A HEARTBEAT

Carolyn's granddaughter, Elissa, has a horse named Princess. Elissa lives on a ranch and boards horses to help pay for her education.

Perhaps a love for horses is in the Miles genes! Cindy and Elissa's ancestral grandfather Miles was a stable boy for the queen of England before he hid out on a ship and came to America.

ELISSA AND PRINCESS

Carolyn's son, Jeff and his family, have a fluffy cat named Marshmallow who loves to have Grandma Carolyn come to visit. He jumps onto her shoulder and combs her hair with his paw and his tongue.

Carolyn's son, Rick and his wife, Janine have a Golden Doodle named Miller. Miller loves company and brings all of his toys to share with them.

Mike's daughter, Jessica and her family, have two dogs to play with and love their boys, Gannon, Beckett and Andersen, a Chocolate Lab named Roxie and a Boston Terrier, English Bulldog mix, named Lola. Gannon has an aquarium in his room.

Beckie's daughter, Nickie and her family have a beautiful German Shepherd named Ryker. Ryker was born in Yugoslavia and trained to protect their family.

RYKER WITH JUSTIN AND BROOKE

Beckie's son Taylor had a dog named Max when he was a little boy. The painting I did of them portrays the love they felt for one another.

MAX AND HIS BOY TAYLOR

My son, Bob and his family, have a Siamese cat named just Kitty and a Chihuahua dog, named Chico. I did a painting of Bob and Tracee's daughter, Mayla with Chico.

MAYLA AND CHICO

My only great great grandchild, Tinley, has two Great Danes, Axle and Lila to love and protect her.

I am so thankful that pets are very important in the lives of my children and grandchildren.

Although dogs and cats are probably the most popular pets, there are many others: horses, pigs rabbits, hamsters, guinea pigs, turtles and even snakes that have shown love and devotion to their owners, helping them slow down and lead a more simple life.

A recent news report told of a working dog called a "Calming Dog" who was brought into a crowded airline terminal to help calm passengers whose flights had been cancelled. It might be said that dogs are working to create a safer, calmer environment for humans.

Our Grandma Edick had a parakeet named Petie, who could say only two words –"pretty bird". Petie sat on Grandma's shoulder and picked bits of food from her mouth! I don't think that I could love a bird quite that much, but my Tousie gives me lots of wet kisses on my mouth –and I love it. One of Grandma's friends had a parrot who entertained her by singing, "My Wild Irish Rose."

My cousins, Mat and Janice, have a pet pig named Leadbelly. In Janice's words, "Leadbelly follows me everywhere I go. She loves to talk (she never shuts up) and does tricks for me, like drinking out of a cup. She loves to play with any old blanket. One morning I was taking a nap on the couch and I awoke to her nuzzling my chin. She had pushed the door open and come into the house to let me know that she loved me. Her favorite foods are bologna and cheese sandwiches and pears. When I am not being a good Mom and paying attention to her, she likes to nip me on the foot. Leadbelly makes a great pillow for star gazing and cloud watching. One night we had some strangers who came in the middle of the night. They were up to no good, but they got the surprise of their criminal lives when they broke into our garage and Leadbelly attacked them."

LEADBELLY

This painting might have been of the Lebow cabin on the Kansas prairie 1883. Orley Lebow, a distant relative, was only a few weeks old when a blizzard hit the area lasting for days. With no more fuel for the coal-wood stove and part of their furniture having been burned, it was still many degrees below zero in the cabin. The family milk cow was brought into the cabin to help warm it and baby Orley was placed on the cow's udder to keep him warm and save his life.

PIONEERS

My late husband, Bob, often told me about his pet goat but it wasn't until recently that I was given an old photo album that held a picture of Bob and his goat, taken in Winslow, Arizona ca 1918. I was inspired to do this painting "The Kid's Breakfast."

THE KID'S BREAKFAST

My painting of a little black girl with a white German Shepherd was on an easel in my living room when the minister from my church came to visit. He asked, "Why did you make her black?" I replied that I wanted to learn how to do different skin colors. I have often wondered why I didn't answer, "And why shouldn't I have chosen to make her black?" Unlike many humans, dogs do not choose between black and white to show their love.

TRUE LOVE

When Arlene's step-son, Benjamin, a fifteen-year old came to live with her and his Grandpa Gary, he had to leave his dog behind. Grandma and Grandpa found a new dog for him, a five-week old female American Bulldog. Benjamin chose the puppy's name, Pearl, since it was December 7th, 2002.

Benjamin was away from home a lot and when he left the nest at age eighteen, Pearl became Gary's dog. Arlene went to work every day and left Gary sleeping. The minute Arlene was out of the house, Pearl was on Arlene's pillow snuggling up to Gary.

Arlene was a runner and Pearl ran with her. One morning, after their walk, Arlene fell and broke her leg. Having a cell phone with her, she called for help. Pearl sat by her head until the ambulance arrived.

When Arlene's eight month old grandson, Levi, was crawling, faster than Grandma could keep up, Pearl would stand guard at the top of the open basement stairwell. When Levi came too close, she would side up to him and push him back to safety.

When Grandpa Gary became very ill and was on his deathbed, Pearl jumped upon the bed and refused to leave, Hours after Grandpa had breathed his last breath. Pearl had to be lifted down. Now Pearl became Grandma Arlene's dog and took trips out of town in the motor coach. She did a good job of keeping strangers away.

It was December, 2013, when there was no hope of Pearl recovering from a tumor. Arlene asked her brothers to accompany her to the Bark Ave. Hospital. Arlene held Pearl and she just put her head down and went to sleep forever.

EVERYONE NEEDS A PEARL

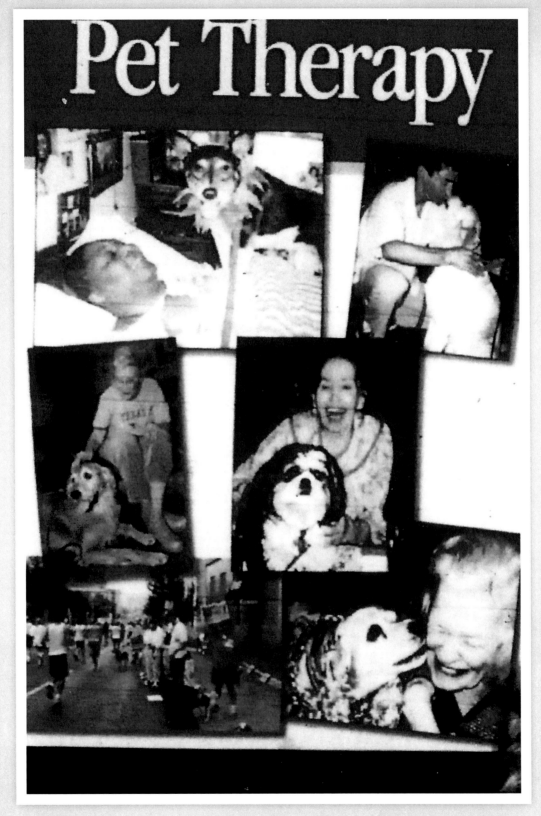

PET THERAPY

My name is Mimi. My owner is Dane. We are members of the Therapy Pet Pal organization in Houston, Texas. We visit hospitals and nursing homes in the area to brighten the days for the patients and residents in Houston, Texas.

Cardiologist Stephen Senalia, M.D. says, "Surgery patients who cuddle with a pet after surgery receive a rush of pain-relieving endorphins and need 50% less pain medication."

MIMI

Aldene was in an auto accident and left paralyzed. She lived In a nursing home for thirty years and has since passed on. Aldene loved Mimi so much. Mimi would lie on the bed with Aldene and lick her hands feet and face. Aldene would say over and over, "Mimi, I love you, I love you." Many can relate to a dog's affection more easily than to affection from a human.

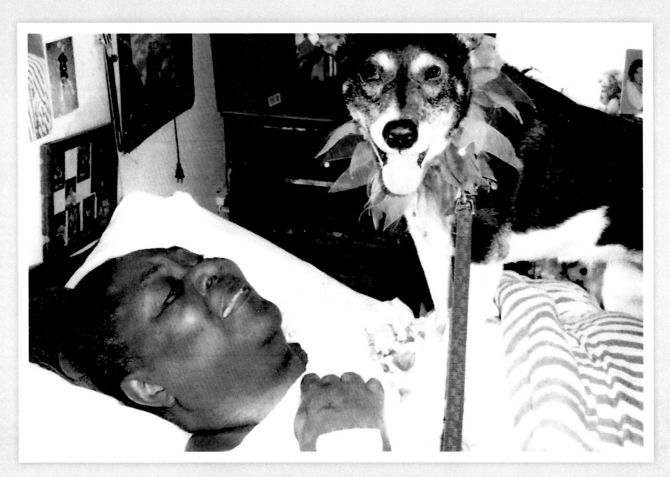

ALDENE AND MIMI

Champ, a Labrador Retriever is a working dog at the Anne Carlsen Center at Jamestown, North Dakota. He works with handicapped children and young adults, ages four to twenty-one, helping them toward their full potential in many aspects of life.

Individuals with Autism Spectrum Disorder have a difficult time dealing with transaction. Champ is trained to help them overcome reluctance and frustration and to gain more self- confidence.

The students at Anne Carlsen Center have come to love Champ and their eyes light up when he approaches to help them walk to lunch or to have them brush or pet him. The grooming not only provides soothing comfort to the children, but also allows them to use a range of motions that loosen up their muscles.

CHAMP

CHAMP

TOUSIE

I lost Tina when she was twelve and a few months later I found Tousie, another Westie, in a newspaper ad. It was after my near-fatal auto accident and during the time I was trying to graduate from a wheel chair and a walker to a cane. I would walk from my chair to the back door to take Tousie to her leash, then back to my chair where I dropped my cane. She often grabbed my cane and ran with it, forcing me to walk without it. I like to say that she helped me learn to walk again,

Tousie loves me unconditionally. She seems to understand a lot of what I say, perhaps it is my tone of voice or could it be that animals are not "dumb animals" after all? They are much more intelligent than we give them credit for being.

Tousie watches over me as a mother watches over her child. She lets me know when it is time to eat (of course I share with her) and when it is time to go to bed. She looks at me as if to say, "Mom, it is past bedtime." If I ignore her, after a while, she goes into bed by herself. She sleeps on a pillow in back of my pillow. After playtime and my often telling her what lucky girls we are to have one another, she gives me a kiss on the forehead, settles onto her pillow with her little black nose in my hair and says, "Aah." When we lived in Mesa, Tousie loved to sit in front of the sliding glass doors where she could watch cars coming on the nearby street. She recognized those cars belonging to family and close friends and would run back and forth from me, in my recliner, to the front door until they arrived. She also seems to recognize voices on the phone and reacts in the same way, expecting them to ring the doorbell. I'm not sure how she knows; perhaps it is the recognition of voices or is it my words to the caller, such as, "See you soon." that give her a clue?

If I sleep in too late, even though she can go into the backyard by way of her pet door, she stands by my bed and barks at me until I answer, "O.K., Tousie, I'll get up and start the day."

When I spend extra time doing my hair and makeup and put on my shoes, Tousie knows that either I am going out or that we are having company. She runs to the front door and waits if I say, "We have company coming," or "Beckie is coming."

When I go out she anticipates the treats I always give her with the words, "You be a good girl Tousie and take care of our house until I get back." She settles in her favorite spot and is always at the door with a wagging tail to welcome me home.

As I approach my ninetieth birthday, I could almost be called a "shut in". Sometimes a week goes by when I don't talk to another human, except by phone. The conversations I have with my Tousie keep me from getting lonely. Animals somehow seem to rise above a bad situation and make the best of every day. Just as Ruth's adopted feline family attributed to her health and happiness in the later years of her life, so does my faithful canine companion, Tousie, add love, happiness and a sense of being needed to the winter years of my life.

Printed in the United States
By Bookmasters